SWORN

Friendship in a Fragile World

Christo ᴧus' Southard

with Peter D. Reed, Sr.

SWORN Foundation, Inc.
790 Juno Ocean Walk Suite 102
Juno Beach, FL 33408

Friendship is the only cement that will
ever hold the world together.

Woodrow Wilson

This book is dedicated to…

Keegan Southard, Caleb Southard, Peter Reed, Jr.
and the future husband of Jaden Southard

If no one else reads it, we're okay with that, but we're
hoping a few more will…

Contents

Introduction

It was 9:00PM on a Sunday evening. Our youth group meeting had ended and Lance and I were reflecting on the night in the Coffee House at First Presbyterian. Somehow the conversation turned to friendship.

I commented that his friendship with Karl and Kyle seemed solid. He agreed and asked me about my friends. After describing my relationship with a few guys, Lance interrupted, "Wow, you don't have any friends."

I thought to myself, "You little punk kid, what do you know?" I attempted to explain that I did, but as I fumbled around to make a case, I realized he was right. (Lance you're still a punk, but thanks, bro.)

That experience resulted in a personal journey for me. It began a hunt for true friendship, a desire to find some buds to do life with. Since that night, I have had the privilege of developing and deepening some very solid "Sworn" friendships over the years. You know who you are. Thanks!

One of those friends is Peter Reed. This book has been a three year journey. It is truly the fruit of a Sworn friendship. As I write, we are heading into our final edit. Our friendship began with an introduction.

It was roughly five years ago when Bill Fleming, President - Palm Beach Atlantic University (PBA), introduced me, Peter Reed, to my now Sworn friend, Chris 'Suds' Southard. It was a chance meeting. Bill knowing where I was in my journey made it a point to initiate the connection to Suds, PBA Men's Lacrosse Coach. Suds was outwardly engaging in his reception that December morning on the steps of the Greene Sports Complex. I've come to believe it was a spiritual connection and that God knew what I needed at this time in my life, a Sworn brother.

The day I met Peter, I had come to a place where God had invited me to pay closer attention to my friendships with men. I had come to the realization that for most of my life, I had not truly experienced the type of Sworn friendship that David and Jonathan experience in the Bible. It was easy to experience shallow connections being in full-time ministry. Although there was potential for real, sacred friendships spoken about in the Bible, for years I was unable to engage with other men because of barriers in my own soul and walls around my heart. I had recently experienced a deepening friendship with God, and the table had been set for a meal with Peter. Our first bro-date was breakfast at Too Jays.

It had been a month or so after I met Suds when he invited me to breakfast. He wanted to thank me for a gift I had given to the PBA Men's Lacrosse Program. I've never been one to share my inner anguish, especially with another man. God had been speaking to my heart. I was in the midst of my divorce and for some reason I felt compelled to share some of what I was going through. I spoke of some of the pain I experienced as a child when my parents got divorced. I was concerned that our divorce would impact my son's life and ever change our family unit. It was as if the flood gates had opened, and I was able to begin alleviating years of internal turmoil.

Peter's vulnerability moved me that morning, and it encouraged me to share with him about the death of my son, Joshua. I had come to understand that there were essential ingredients necessary for a sacred friendship to develop between men, and vulnerability was one of them. Both Peter and I have come to believe that the most important ingredient in friendship is one's friendship with God. It was clear that while on different journeys, we both longed to know the heart of God. I sensed a mutual respect for one another.

Over the next few years we fostered our friendship. We partnered on several ministry missions. Initially we partnered with PBA Men's Lacrosse and Fellowship of Christian Athletes (FCA) Lacrosse. (Thanks J-Moe for your friendship in mission.) We expanded our partnership to include various gatherings of men, as well as mission trips, including a men's trip to Montana, that we have come to affectionately call "The Trip of Seven Brothers," which is where the idea of this book was conceived.

Before the 2016 Seven Brothers Trip, I had texted Suds quoting I Samuel 20:42: "Jonathan said to David, 'Go in peace, for we have Sworn friendship with each other in the LORD.'" It was over a week before Suds responded to the text, wherein he never acknowledged the verse I had previously sent, leading me to wonder if Suds really had a heart for God and if our manaffection had faded.

Unbeknownst to Peter, I had become captivated with the word "Sworn" in the verse he had sent me. I was so consumed that I woke up in the middle of the night, contemplating the word's "Sworn" and "friendship" and how the two intertwine. Eventually, at one of our Brew Brother's Gatherings at Twisted Trunk, I shared with Peter how deeply impacted I was by the passage of scripture he sent me.

Fast forward a month or so, we were journeying to Montana with our seven brothers; Scott, our beekeeping bud Karl, Big Brad, Jonny T, Suds, me, and of course, our seventh brother and Sworn friend, Jesus. (On a side note, the name "Seven Brothers" came from a beer offered at the Black Tooth Brewing Company in Wyoming.) Suds and I bantered and brainstormed on the seven-hour ride from the Denver airport to the Big Horn River in Montana. Sitting in the last row of the sweet mini-van, captained by Jonny T, Sworn, which was going to initially be a cool tee-shirt, then maybe a seminar, but ultimately has become the book, was born.

Our Fragile World

Our world *is* fragile... fragile environment... fragile foreign relations... fragile political system... fragile marriages... fragile friendships...

Our world is fragile, but God is not fragile. He is our Rock and our anchor in stormy seas. God's commitment to "relatedness" can be found in the Old Testament. This is not a fragile commitment, but a Sworn Covenant. He commits Himself to relationships, which is a free sovereign act. God does not waver in this commitment, even though we might. This Sworn Covenant with a fragile world is evident in His relationship with the world and all humanity. God is our model for friendship. God is Sworn. He has Sworn to preserve the friendship He has forged with creation, namely His sons and daughters.

God is friendship. His loyalty can be trusted. God invites us to a sacred friendship in a fragile world. All of us can experience His "Swornness" firsthand. In turn, we can enter this fragile world, arm-in-arm with a friend. Peter Reed became that friend for me, and Chris Southard became that friend to me.

Although we consider this book an attempt at an inspirational comedy, it should provoke you and cause you to pause. If you are willing to contemplate your own frozen sea within your soul, we hope this book awakens you to more profound pain and hope existing in the caverns of your heart. This pain or sense of loneliness, if we give it a name, is healable, but only through the medicinal effects of friendship.

Enjoy the adventure together with a good friend.

Cheers!

Chapter I
Sworn

Jonathan said to David,
"Go in peace for we have a **Sworn** friendship
with each other in the name of the Lord."

I Samuel 20:42

I couldn't shake that text from my friend Peter. Something was birthed that day, a new seed of contemplation. What was this friendship between Jonathan and David? How did it begin? Develop? And mature? So began a journey with a friend to discover the answers to these questions. It started with a closer look at Jonathan and David's relationship as friends in the Lord.

Text - from Peter to Suds...
Saturday, September 3, 2016, 8:14AM

Jonathan said to David, "Go in peace for we have Sworn friendship with each other in the name of the Lord." I Samuel 20:42. I read this verse and thought of you. I hope you and your family have a great Labor Day Weekend.

Peter had shared a bit of mantimacy with me.

The first lesson in Sworn friendship: don't take nine days to respond. And as any Sworn friend would do, Peter was not bashful in letting me know. In fact, that conversation about text etiquette in the back of the van in 2016 was when we first started talking about writing this book.

Response text from Suds to Peter
Monday, September 12, 2016, 5:58PM

Hey, Brother... I have a book for you... can you do the twisted trunk tomorrow night?

Crickets!

Follow up text from Suds to Peter
Monday, September 12, 2016, 8:11PM

Jonathan said to David, "Go in peace for we have Sworn friendship with each other in the name of the Lord." I Samuel 20:42

Peter's Response text...timely...
Monday, September 12, 2016, 9:38PM

Not sure on the twisted trunk...

Ice... Ice... Baby... We eventually got that beer...

It began with a close look at Jonathan and David's relationship.

David, a shepherd boy, slayer of giants and future leader of Israel, first meets Jonathan, son of King Saul, on the battlefield. Jonathan witnesses young David carrying the head of the Philistines' fallen champion Goliath, who he had just overcome with a mere slingshot stone to the head.

We've come to believe that friendships are often conceived with first impressions. Jonathan was undoubtedly impressed with David's conquest so much so that the "soul of Jonathan was knit to the soul of David."

Friendship at First Sight

You may be impressed with someone's accomplishments, sense of humor, appearance, stature in the community, knowledge, etc. Like an iceberg where only ten percent (10%) is visual; this is the surface of friendship.

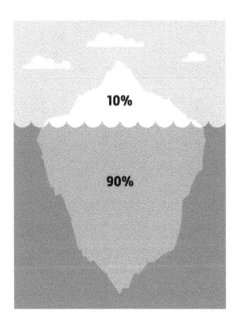

We believe a decision is made relatively quickly in one's mind as to whether this person is worth pursuing further along the road to Sworn friendship. Almost like dating, or what is now referred to as "bromance."

Although these initial impressions could be construed as superficial, the perceptions fuel the desire to continue to explore the potential friendship. Without these intriguing first impressions, friendship runs the risk of not advancing.

Every friendship begins somewhere, at some time. For the friendship to mature, a commitment must be made by both parties for it to flourish.

The idea of a Sworn or "Sacred" friendship involves more than a passing encounter. By necessity, it develops with an internal oath or covenant that both friends agree upon.

It is confirmed when two friends refuse to go away. They become steadfast in their commitment to one another. They "cut" a covenant of expectation. It goes beyond being fishing buddies, golfing buddies, or whatever kind of buddies. It goes beyond friends who buy connections or, in other words, "friends with benefits." They begin to walk on the path of a Sworn friendship. Their souls are in the process of being knit together.

> And Jonathan made a covenant with David because he loved him as himself. Jonathan took off the robe he was wearing and gave it to David, along with his tunic, and even his sword, his bow, and his belt. Whatever mission Saul sent him on, David was so successful that Saul gave him a high rank in the army. This pleased all the troops, and Saul's officers as well.

I Samuel 18:3-5

A desire grows for the other to increase in wisdom, stature, and in favor with God and man, as Jesus did.

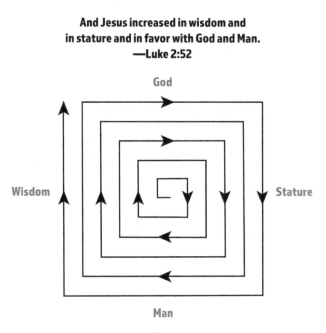

And Jesus increased in wisdom and in stature and in favor with God and Man.
—Luke 2:52

God

Wisdom

Stature

Man

Loyalty

Saul told his son Jonathan and all the attendants to kill David. But Jonathan had taken a great liking to David and warned him, "My father Saul is looking for a chance to kill you. Be on your guard tomorrow morning; go into hiding and stay there. I will go out and stand with my father in the field where you are. I'll speak to him about you and will tell you what I find out." Jonathan spoke well of David to Saul, his father, and said to him, "Let not the king do wrong to his servant David; he has not wronged you, and what he has done has benefited you greatly. He took his life in his hands when he killed the Philistine. The LORD won a great victory for all Israel, and you saw it and were glad. Why then would you do wrong to an innocent man like David by killing him for no reason?" Saul listened to Jonathan and took this oath: "As surely as the LORD lives, David will not be put to death." So Jonathan called David and told him the whole conversation. He brought him to Saul, and David was with Saul as before.

I Samuel 19:1-7

As David's fame rose, King Saul's jealousy rose as well, and as a result, David fell from favor in the eyes of King Saul.

An aspect of Sworn friendship is played out. We believe that an essential ingredient in this type of friendship is loyalty. Jonathan is clearly loyal to David, so much so that he opposes his father and chooses his friend over his father. Loyalty is a gift of friendship. It is a gift that cannot be demanded; however, without it, there is no Sworn friendship. Loyalty is given as an act of friendship. Jonathan was compelled, by his internal covenant, to persuade his father, King Saul, to reconsider his intentions against David. This kind of act is evidence of a seasoned and developed friendship.

Loyalty, like any other virtue, comes at a price. One fruit of a Sworn friendship is the peace that comes with knowing that the friend would always look after the family of the friend in a time of need or crisis. The friend would have no hesitation asking the friend. It goes without saying.

David's Kindness to Mephibosheth (Jonathan's Son)

And David said, "Is there still anyone left of the house of Saul, that I may show him kindness for Jonathan's sake?" Now there was a servant of the house of Saul whose name was Ziba, and they called him to David. And the king said to him, "Are you Ziba?" And he said, "I am your servant." And the king said, "Is there not still someone of the house of Saul, that I may show the kindness of God to him?" Ziba said to the king, "There is still a son of Jonathan; he is crippled in his feet." The king said to him, "Where is he?" And Ziba said to the king, "He is in the house of Machir, the son of Ammiel, at Lo-debar." Then King David sent and brought him from the house of Machir the son of Ammiel, at Lo-debar. And Mephibosheth the son of Jonathan, son of Saul, came to David and fell on his face and paid homage. And David said, "Mephibosheth!" And he answered, "Behold, I am your servant." And David said to him, "Do not fear, for I will show you kindness for the sake of your father Jonathan, and I will restore to you all the land of Saul, your father, and you shall eat at my table always." And he paid homage and said, "What is your servant, that you should show regard for a dead dog such as I?"

Then the king called Ziba, Saul's servant, and said to him, "All that belonged to Saul and to all his house I have given to your master's grandson. And you and your sons and your servants shall till the land for him and shall bring in the produce, that your master's grandson may have bread to eat. But Mephibosheth, your master's grandson shall always eat at my table." Now Ziba had fifteen sons and twenty servants. Then Ziba said to the king, "According to all that, my lord, the king commands his servant, so will your servant do." So Mephibosheth ate at David's[a] table, like one of the king's sons. And Mephibosheth had a young son, whose name was Mica. And all who lived in Ziba's house became Mephibosheth's servants. So Mephibosheth lived in Jerusalem, for he always ate at the king's table. Now he was lame in both his feet.

II Samuel 9: 1-13

A friend never forgets the family of a friend. Never!

Six Essential Ingredients of a Sworn Friendship

Before we even load the chamber with the six essential ingredients of a Sworn friendship, we feel we need to say that without investing **effort and time**, a Sworn friendship is not sustainable. We realize that time is spent in various ways on life commitments and demands; with that said, we have come to believe that you must make time for things you value. As Socrates said, "Of all possessions, the most precious is a good and sincere friend."[1] We both believe, Peter and I, that Socrates was spot on. We are experiencing the ripening and maturing fruit in our journey together as friends. We continue to be intentional with our effort and time, the bowl and mixing spoon of friendship

Round 1: Friendship with God

Come near to God, and He will come near to you.

James 4:8

James describes a longing for God's felt presence, a deep God connection:

A deepening, ongoing friendship with God is filled with conversational light-heartedness. It is an experience free of shame, guilt, and fear. It is fresh and life-giving. As Moses exclaimed in Exodus 33:18, "Please show me your glory."

The majestic God of the universe has gone to great lengths to enjoy a sacred friendship with us. "For God so loved the world that he gave His one and only son, that whoever believes in Him will not perish, but will have eternal life." (John 3:16)

We are fully aware that guys are in different places in their understanding of God as a Friend, Father, Guide. We respect the fact that men are on a journey filled with questions, disappointments, and confusion concerning their relationship with God. Nevertheless, we believe that God desires to have a friendship with us. It has been said that God is love, but it also can be said that God is friendship.

God has created man with a longing for Himself. Augustine has written, "You have made us for yourself, and our heart is restless until it rests in You."[2] This restlessness or longing for God fuels our desire to begin and maintain a friendship with God. What does this friendship look like, you ask? It is the fullness of good times and memorable experiences shared with great friends. It's laughter, tears, joy, sorrow, unforgettable memories. It's the pearl of great price. There is a progression to our friendship with God. Time and everyday experiences together will fortify and invigorate this relationship. This friendship cannot and will not ever become dull or played out if it has been given the attention and time it needs to flourish.

William A. Barry, SJ, describes this developing friendship:

> Once we get over the kind of fear of God engendered by early training, we enter something like a honeymoon period with God. This is followed by a period of distance when we recognize how shamefully short we have fallen of God's hopes for us. The distance is closed when we realize that God loves us, warts and sins and all, and the friendship is solidified. We are able to be ourselves with God. Ultimately, we can become collaborators with God in God's family business. For Christians, this stage of collaboration in the family business is called discipleship, or friendship with Jesus of Nazareth. Finally, friendship with Jesus, as all Christians know, ultimately leads to facing with him his horrible death on the cross.
>
> **William A. Barry**[3]

As the children in the *Chronicles of Narnia* asked the Narnians, what Aslan (God figure) is like, they responded: "He is good, but he is not safe." Many of us need to have our image of God healed. God created us in his image, and we return the favor of creating Him in our image. Often, we expect God to be a superhero, immediately showing up in our time of need. We chide Him for his apparent no show and accuse Him of not hearing our cries for help. With these false expectations of God, the plumb-line which set our foundation is off, which leads to the eventual collapse of our relationship with God. Our God suffers with us, and therefore, He invites us to carry our own crosses with the courage He provides. He is good, but He is not safe. He is just, but He is also our friend.

Jesus helps to heal our false assumptions of God, and as He does, it makes friendship with God possible. God referred to Moses and Abraham as friends.

> Thus the Lord used to speak to Moses face to face, as a man speaks to his friend.

Exodus 33:11

> But you, Israel, my servant, Jacob, whom I've have chosen, the offspring of Abraham, my friend.

Isaiah 41:8

> And the scripture was fulfilled that said, Abraham believed God, and was counted to him as righteousness... and he was called a friend of God.

James 2:23

Jesus also said, "If you have seen me, you have also seen the Father." Jesus progressed in his relationship with his disciples, where he said, "I no longer call you servants, I call you friends."

Friendship with God is necessary for human friendship. They impact each other.

> If anyone says, "I love God," yet hates his brother, he is a liar. For anyone who does not love his brother, whom he has seen, cannot love God, whom he has not seen. And he has given us this command: Whoever loves God must also love his brother.
>
> **I John 4:20-21**

> My commandment is this: Love each other as I have loved you. Greater love has no one than this that he lay down his life for his friends.
>
> **I John 15:12-13**

As the friendship with God grows, the potential for greater intimacy with another increases. "Deep calls to deep," the Sworn friendship we are writing about runs parallel with our Sworn friendship with God.

When my (Suds) spiritual journey took a significant turn in college, I came to realize that the Father of Jesus had great affection for me. A monk once said that from time to time The Father seizes us with "the power of great affection." He then went on to say that when that occurs, "please notify your face." Understanding God's love for me has been a challenge. Trusting Him has been an even more significant challenge. But like a good Father, He continues to display his affection when I need it most.

Early in my journey, I was invited to a charismatic church service by my first Sworn friend, Ian Russell. Ian had been instrumental in helping me see that the present path I was on didn't end happily. It was my junior year in college, and Ian was the guy that God sent to enable me to move from distrust of Christians and Christianity to trust. So when he invited me to the church he attended I accepted because, in many ways, he had "earned the right to be heard" and "clearly showed me how much he cared before he told me how much he knew." (Both memorable quotes I learned from Young Life, a ministry that befriends high school students.)

This was my first charismatic gig full of high powered worship, prophetic speech, and lots of glossolalia (speaking in tongues). I was raised Catholic, so this church experience caused my mouth to drop wide open, and my butt cheeks to clench. Where were the wafers and wine, kneelers, and elaborately robed priests? Instead, the place was seemingly full of new wine, pew jumpers, and a dude in a Hawaiian shirt. I was familiar with the story of the Guyana cult, so I was waiting for them pass the Jim Jones juice, which was what my buddies and I referred to as the Everclear and punch we served at our lax parties. These folks were definitely drunk, but I'm pretty sure they were drunk in the Spirit, except for this guy sitting next to me who smelled like a Rum Runner (or was that me, as I had been out partying the night before). The end of the service arrives, and the Preacher in the Hawaiian shirt invites people to pray out loud in their "prayer language." I turned to Ian and said, "Prayer what!?" I was struggling to pray in English, let alone another language. He briefly explained to me that the language was a gift from the Holy Spirit. I thought to myself, "Awesome, but how does one secure one's gift, and can it be Spanish because I'm sitting on a D in Spanish presently." For the time being, Ian encouraged me to pray in English, and so I did.

Later, any person who wanted to receive a "prayer language" was invited into a back room. Now I was in full commando mode… "What's behind door #1? A little Jim Jones juice?" Okay, it had just gotten weird, but I trusted Ian, so I went. My heart was open to whatever God had for me, so I was up for any and all adventures He encouraged me to take. They ushered us in a line, singing the God Congo Song (just Sudsing with you). They had us stand side by side as prayer counselors walked among us, encouraging us to open our mouths and simply speak whatever came out. First, the person to the left of me started talking. I think something like Mandarin Chinese and the person to the right of me began to pray in some kind of alien tongue I recognized from *Star Trek*. Something like Vulcan. This dude was boldly going where no man had gone before…

When my turn came, as not to feel left out, I said, "Hola, Jesus, cómo estás?" because nothing else wanted to come out. Then something wonderful, mysterious, and organic happened. I began to say or pray two similar sounding words; shelemiah and shelumiel. I began to repeat those words over and over and felt the power of His great affection and a sense of deep peace. Later that night, I arrived back on campus and opened my study Bible to see if I could somehow find these words and potentially their meaning. I turned to the Biblical Encyclopedia Index, and there they were on page 273. They were both Hebrew words. Shelemiah means "at peace with God," and Shelumiel means "friend of Yahweh." That changed everything for me. God was inviting me to experience His peace and friendship, the two things I needed most.

Round 2: Common Interests

> Friendship arises out of mere companionship when two or more of the companions discover that they have in common some insight or interest which the others do not share.
>
> **CS Lewis**[4]

The common interest that ignited our friendship was our love for the Native American game, or as it's referred to: The Creators Game, lacrosse. When President Fleming introduced us, Suds was the Men's Lacrosse Coach at Palm Beach Atlantic University. My son was playing high school lacrosse. Bill was aware of our common interest and subsequently made the connection. This interest provided some common ground and enabled us to begin the possibility of friendship. We shared our love of watching our son's play. Suds was able to coach my son, Peter Jr., on an FCA travel lacrosse team, and I would often stand with Suds on the sideline. I was loud and amusingly involved in the game, frequently yelling lacrosse "Reedisms" like "Cherish the ball!" or "Deuce-him!" We would take notes on what we had to work on improving with our sons, which is a common issue for dads who are re-living their sports careers through their kids. We were good at reminding each other it was only a game and afterward would try to tell our sons that we just loved watching them play… period. Suds saying, "I'd scrap my game notes for a hug and pat on the back."

Later, Peter got involved in mentoring with some players from the PBA lacrosse team. We define mentoring as a more mature individual spending thought-filled time listening and sharing wisdom with another. I have always been committed to the proverb "iron sharpens iron" as it pertains to the maturity of an individual. "Iron sharpens iron" describes the process by which two individuals share life in such a way that together their lives are honed and strengthened. Peter shared that interest in leadership development, as well as the "iron sharpens iron" philosophy.

Someone once asked Coach Joe Ehrmann, "How is your team going to be this year?"

He responded with, "I'll let you know in five years."

Our friendship led to a partnership in walking with our sons, but also young college men as they navigated the often-treacherous terrain of life. We have made a lot of mistakes along the way and hoped to share our collective wisdom.

Common interests led to a common mission, which produced a deep sense of fulfillment as we've journeyed to be Sworn friends.

Round 3: Loyalty

> A man of many companions may come to ruin, but there is a friend who sticks closer than a brother.
>
> **Proverbs 18:24**

Friendship in our day is often spoken about in terms of Facebook-friends, business-friends, fishing-friends, etc. Although there may be a particular loyalty in those relationships, the loyalty we speak about in a Sworn friendship is a Holy different type. And yes, we meant to say "Holy" because the depth of this loyalty is incomparable. It is uniquely set apart, God-given, and sustained.

The friend who sticks closer than a brother can be counted on as steadfast and trustworthy. The biblical example of Jonathan and David was a closer-than-brothers bond. They went through many trials and tribulations together, yet their "Swornness" remained. Jonathan risked his life for David, the ultimate test of loyalty. Now we're not suggesting you need to take a bullet for a Sworn friend, but you might.

My loyalty toward Peter played out during a mission trip to an under-resourced community in the Dominican Republic. The sanitation system in this community was an elevated containment channel or stream that flows through the community collecting waste runoff from homes. Subsequently, we have named this "Pooh River," and there was unfortunately no honey flowing from this jar. The area had recently experienced torrential rains as it does in the summer months, which caused the "Pooh River" to be uncharacteristically high. As we journeyed through the community, we came across a bridge that took you across "Pooh River."

Whatever, Suds. You can call it a bridge, but most people would call it a balance beam made of broken bricks crossing a sea of human excrement. And I'm not sure if Moses would have parted this one.

Our guide, a youthful local boy, skipped across the beam-like bridge as graceful as a seasoned gymnast. The mission team members, one by one, crossed in single file as the wastewater began to flow over the top of the now slick bricks.

When Peter's turn came, he turned to me and said, "What the…"—insert your favorite expletive—"did you get me into here, Suds?" At just a third of the way across, Peter froze with fear. Fear, a term Peter likes to refer to as "false events appearing real."

NO, THIS WAS REAL… if I fell, I was looking at more than a 30-foot drop to the west into very tough terrain, resulting in multiple broken bones and lacerations, or to the east into the waste containment system of "Pooh River," resulting in flesh disintegration and mutation caused by biohazardous toxic waste. As any loyal friend would, Suds began to hum a verse from his favorite Christmas cartoon song, "Put one foot in front of the other…"

As Peter emerged from his paralysis, he began to shuffle like a 90-year-old man across the bridge-like beam. Now mid-way across, Peter demanded that I carry his backpack as he believed it would cause him to lose his balance and fall. As Peter continued with his expletive-filled shuffle, I nearly fell in myself from laughing so much.

After crossing the river, I (Peter) found myself thanking God for his loyalty, but questioning my Sworn friend Suds for getting me into such a situation, but I remained ultimately thankful, nevertheless.

A note on the Dominican Republic: I've led over twenty mission trips to the DR working on projects like roads, homes, bridges, and water purification plants. Peter has joined me on several of those trips. The above story is funny as we recall it, but what isn't funny is how we take for granted our lives here in the States. As we mentioned several times in this book, true friendship gives birth to mission. We are called to "go" and serve the world God called us to "belong" to. We belong to God and therefore we belong to one another. Thanks, Cristian Santiago, for reminding us that, "First we demonstrate the Gospel, then we proclaim it." You have been a solid Sworn friend for many years. Thanks, Hermano!

Round 4: Vulnerability

> To share your weakness is to make yourself vulnerable, to make yourself vulnerable is to show your strength.
>
> **Criss Jami**

Guys in today's society are not wired for vulnerability. Why? Is that because we are afraid to show weakness? Or is it that we have been conditioned to avoid sharing our hearts?

Many men have decided that feeling is unnecessary… that having an open heart just sets you up for hurt and pain.

We will discuss the need for emotional intimacy in a Sworn friendship in an upcoming chapter, but for now, II Corinthians 12:9-10 captures the importance of men being vulnerable. "But he said to me, 'my grace is sufficient for you, for my power is made perfect in weakness.' Therefore I will boast all the more gladly of my weakness, so that the power of Christ may rest upon me. For the sake of Christ, then, I am content with weakness, insults hardships, persecutions, and calamities. For when I am weak, then I am strong."

Round 5: Equality

> Friendship either finds equals or makes them. Where there is inequality, one takes pre-eminence and the other bares subjection.
>
> **Jerome**[5]

In *Spiritual Friendship*, Aelred of Rievaulx informs us, "It is also a law of friendship that the superior must be on a plane of equality with the inferior... therefore in friendship... let the lofty descend, the lowly ascend; the rich be in want, the poor become rich; and thus let each communicate his condition to the other, so that equality may be the result." [6]

In our study of Jonathan and David, we found equality to be present in this friendship, as Jonathan, an heir to the throne, invited a lowly shepherd boy to be his Sworn friend. They established a covenant with each other referred to in I Samuel 18:3 that spanned a generation. This peer-to-peer friendship matured to the point where Jonathan loved David as himself. So clearly, the essential ingredient of "equality" enables us to have reciprocity in our relationship. Equality also, in our opinion, fosters the probability of longevity as the Sworn friend becomes another self.

One main point that comes out clearly in this understanding of friendship is "reciprocity and mutuality." Friends wish each other well and love each other. Augustine brings out this quality of reciprocity and mutuality in friendship when he writes:

> ...to talk and to laugh with them; to do friendly acts of service for one another; to read well-written books together; sometimes to tell jokes and sometimes to be serious; to disagree at times, but without hard feelings, just as a man does with himself; and to keep our many discussions pleasant by the very rarity of such differences; to teach things to the others and to learn from them. To long impatiently for those who were absent, and to receive with joy those joining us. These and similar expressions, proceeding from the hearts of those who loved and repaid their comrade's love, by way of countenance, tongue, eyes, and a thousand pleasing gestures, were like fuel to set our minds ablaze and to make but one out of many.

Confessions IV, 13[7]

Shared experiences, mutuality, and reciprocity enable a deepening sense of equality, and unity grows to make the friendship one out of many.

Round 6: Self-Awareness

Self-Awareness–noun. Conscious knowledge of one's own character, feelings, motives, and desires.

Since the Greek age, "know thyself" has been the rallying cry for the commitment to self-awareness. In Western society, self-awareness has consistently been a subject talked about and contemplated by philosophers and sociologists. The process of self-awareness takes place when one can step back and take an objective view of one's self as it relates to behaviors in real-time.

Socrates has said, "The unexamined life is not worth living." The ability to engage in self-awareness practices makes life worthwhile, especially in the arena of friendship. It is difficult to be friends with someone who is not self-aware because they lack the ability to monitor interactions, good or bad, with the one they long to grow in friendship. When one fails in self-awareness, it becomes nearly impossible to care for one's own soul, not to mention the soul of a friend.

Gregory the Great defines friendship as a commitment to be the guardian of another's soul. II Corinthians 13:5 exhorts us to: "Examine yourself, to see whether you are in the faith. Test yourself. Or do you not realize this about yourselves, that Jesus Christ is in you?" So without self-awareness, friendship fails to flourish and eventually fails. Self-awareness is a non–negotiable

A classic parting Reedism is "keep in touch with yourself." Although it is said in different ways, friendship with yourself is a form of self-awareness. It truly is keeping in touch with ones' self. The Psalms are full of personal conversations that David had with himself. For instance, "Why are you cast down, oh my soul?" In a way, it's a form of self-coaching. When we pause and listen to our selves/souls, we enter a quiet place of safety as we work out our internal knots. In that space, there is an opportunity to get in touch with our true selves. So, keep in touch with yourself…

Chapter III
Definition, Types, Conditions, and Stages of Sworn Friendship

A day without a friend is like a pot without a single drop of honey left inside.

Winnie-the-Pooh

Friendship has fallen on hard times. The type of friendship we refer to in this book, Sworn friendship, only survives because it is held together by at least six essential ingredients.

In classical Greek writings, as well as 12th Century Monasticism, the subject of friendship was often spoken about, contemplated, and written about extensively by well-known individuals like Aristotle, Cicero, and Aelred of Rievaulx. Nowadays, "a book on friendship means quite often, a collection of short sayings, attractively illustrated, meant as a gift and sold in a convenience store."[1]

Times have changed, and unfortunately, we live in an age that when you meet someone at a social gathering very little time passes before the question is asked: "What do you do?" Instead of enjoying each other for who we are as human beings, we immediately seek to gain information about the other as a human doing. When asked what we do for a living, Suds and I enjoy redirecting the question with the reply of, "I'm a friend." This quite often leads to a much more interesting and insightful conversation.

> Ours is a world in which work has become dominant, and we identify ourselves in terms of what we do (for pay), not who our friends are.
>
> **Gilbert Meilaender**[2]

The Greek Philosopher Aristotle, and we in our own limited capacity to philosophize, agree that Sworn friendship demands that we spend time in the company of the other with all essential ingredients in play. Aristotle often refers to this idea that "friends must have eaten the required pinch of salt together."[3] Sworn friends flavor each other's lives.

Perhaps the reason that friendship has fallen out of favor in Christendom was because a concern arose that exclusive love of a few select friends is contrary to the Christian ethic.

> If you love those who love you, what reward is that? And if you salute only your brethren, what more are you doing than others?
>
> **Luke 6:32**

This most certainly put the brakes on the imbalance placed on Philia, brotherly or exclusive friendship, or preferential bond. Agape, a more universal love of all, took center stage in Christian practice.

We believe that Agape is of extreme importance in life and in faith and will contend that the love of God (Agape) is for all people. God smiles when He thinks of every single human being on the planet (and beyond, if we find out that alien life exists elsewhere).

Nevertheless, we also firmly believe that Philia or a Sworn friendship is essential for us to grow in love for God then for brothers and sisters in the faith and the world around us. In sports, practice is more important than the game. We believe the pursuit of Sworn friendship prepares us for the game, and nowadays, the stakes are high. Men struggle to connect with other men on deeper, intimate, emotionally-necessary levels. Fathers struggle to show affection to their sons and daughters. Many of us are on a journey to find our hearts, not much different from the Tin Man in *The Wizard of Oz*. It's not that we don't have a heart. The problem is that we have found it dangerous and often painful to awaken it, so we often travel through life two-thirds alive, at best, relying on our minds and guts (passions) to propel us forward.

We miss the tender moments with loved ones. They could be occasions of grace-filled with warmth, kindness, and gentleness, but we shy away due to our lack of self-awareness. **Those we long to love, we fail to love as we never truly learned to love.**

The journey of Sworn friendship opens wide this aspect of ourselves as we seek a felt unity and oneness. Jonathan said of David, "Our hearts are knit together" like threads in a fine tapestry. This knitting of two men's hearts is frightening for most men, often because it is misunderstood. We men created a personal prison we have locked ourselves in after receiving wounds at the hand of those we trusted. These wounds can be catastrophic and extremely difficult to heal. I'm confident, because I personally experienced it, that even the deepest wounds can find healing when Sworn friendship (Philia) is given the proper place it deserves in our society.

Definitions of Friendship

Cicero said, "A relationship based on an agreement about all human and divine matters, together with good-will and affection."[4]

BOOM...

Aristotle describes friendship as reciprocated goodwill.[5]

BOOM...

Marcianius's conversion caused Augustine to think about a definition of friendship. He again quoted Cicero that friendship is "agreement with kindliness and affection about things human and divine," but then he added, "in Christ Jesus, our Lord who is our real peace." (Confessions IV, 14, 18)

This was Augustine's definition of true friendship: "We are united to one another as friends through our union with Christ." Ultimately, Augustine says, "The friendship that matters most for us is our friendship with God."

Too long for a boom...

Gregory the Great says in the *Etymologies of Isidore of Seville,* "A friend is the guardian of one's soul, custos animi."

BOOM...

Aelred of Rievaulx says, "Friendship is that virtue, therefore, through which by a covenant of sweetest love, our very spirits are united, and 'from many are made one.'" (Cicero, *On Friendship*, 25.92). Aelred believed that this type of friendship could never end.

Solomon seems to agree with him in this verse from Proverbs: "A friend loves always" (Proverbs 17:17). So he obviously declares that friendship is eternal if it is true, but if it ceases to exist, then although it seemed to exist, it was not true friendship.

Deuteronomy 13:6 refers to a "friend who is as your own soul..."

Modern-day Mystics Suds and Reeder's definition:

Sworn friendship can be defined as a reciprocal and freely agreed upon guardianship of one another's soul with the purpose of unity of spirit, commitment to mission, and shared growth in the sacred journey of friendship with God.

KABOOM...

Different from the classic definitions of friendship, we have purposely included an aspect of friendship that challenges the other friend to actively participate in altruistic adventures. Agape is the universal love that God has for all humanity. Philia describes a more preferential bond between two individuals, which is often referred to as having another self. We believe the mission is to go into all the world and make disciples of all men (Acts 1:8). Sworn friendship challenges the other to be on mission together.

We call it "bromission." A "bromission" demonstrates love in random acts of kindness by being on a mission to the poor and needy and seeking to share the hope of the gospel with the dark and decaying world. Therefore, the purpose of sacred friendship is to cultivate a greater love for others. This is Sworn friendship's end zone.

A quick word about bromission. I was recently in the Keys with my boys and their friend Reilly. We were invited by my buddy Jeremy Grimmett. Jeremy and Chris Ann like to invite folks down to the Keys to enjoy some rest and relaxation along with some great fishing. Big Brad Finch was with us on this adventure. Our day of fishing was filled with adrenaline, hooking up on Mahi, chill time trolling, chasing birds, and having deep conversations about life and God. The deep blue sea was our backdrop and a constant reminder of the vastness of God's creation (we were out about 38 miles and joked about stopping in Cuba for some cigars). It was a successful day, so instead of going out for dinner we decided to cook our catch. The boys washed the boat and cleaned the fish.

Jeremy and Brad marveled at what great men my sons and their friend had turned out to be. Whether they knew it or not, they and many other men had contributed to the raising of my sons. I will always be thankful for that fact. I was in the kitchen creating my own version of the Lobster Reuben. Then I blackened some Grunt, which, to our surprise, was awesome. Brad and Jeremy grilled some Boudin. Then Brad made us all some Mahi and we built our own tacos. It was truly a Man Feast complete with a tiny bit of green stuff.

Late that night, Jeremy and I sat on the back porch and talked about the "Sworn" mission. Jeremy has always loved the idea of adventure discipleship and evangelism. Jeremy and Brad both have the gift of hospitality; they are connectors. That day on the water Jeremy connected with half a dozen guys, just checking in. I thought to myself: *this guy knows what it means to be someone's friend.*

We spoke about how important it was for guys to get away. Fishing the Keys, West Palm Beach, or the Bahamas were perfect locations for creating adventures for guys. The Sworn mission is about creating space for guys to commit to each other in deeper ways and at the same time develop a deeper friendship with God. If you are interested in a fishing adventure, email us we would love to host a group of your friends.

Peter and I are thankful to have guys like Jeremy and Brad on our leadership team. We are truly on a bromission together!

Types of Friendship

Aelred of Rievaulx wrote one of the most important treatises on Spiritual Friendship. He describes three kinds of friendship; carnal, worldly, and spiritual. Aelred most certainly drew from Aristotle, who outlines three types of friendship in his book, *Nicomachean Ethics*.

The first type of friendship Aristotle describes consisted of common interest or pleasure (golfing or fishing buddies).

The second type of friendship consists of friendship based on gaining benefit or advantage in life or work (a friendship of usefulness).

The third describes the friendship of character, which in Aristotle's writings was referred to as a deep, exceptional, or exclusive friendship. This friendship was valuable for its own sake.

Next is one of the longest quotes I've ever seen outside of a text book. I went back and forth with Suds on this one. He won. Time to focus in guys. Aelred will challenge you.

"He's out there Jerry and loving every minute of it."

Kramer from the sitcom *Seinfeld*

Aelred begins his breakdown of three types of friendship: "Let us call one friendship carnal, another worldly, and the third spiritual."

Carnal Friendship

The carnal is created by a conspiracy in vice, the worldly is enkindled by hope of gain, and the spiritual is cemented among the righteous by a likeness of lifestyles and interests. Then by a gesture, a nod, a word, or an act of deference, spirit is captivated by spirit, one is set afire by another, and they are fused into one so that once this degrading pact is struck, each will perform or endure for the other any possible crime or sacrilege. They consider nothing sweeter, they judge nothing more equitable than this friendship, for they think that to wish and not wish the same things is imposed on them by the laws of friendship. Therefore, this friendship is neither undertaken with thoughtfulness nor sanctioned by judgment nor guided by reason. Not observing moderation, not concerned with honesty, disregarding profit, and loss, it rushes into everything without forethought or discretion but with frivolous excess. Hence, as if hounded by the Furies, it either exhausts itself or disappears into the mist from which it was formed.

Worldly Friendship

Worldly friendship, begotten of greed for temporal goods or for wealth, is always marked by fraud and deception. Here nothing is reliable, constant, or fixed. For worldly friendship fluctuates with fortune and chases coin. Hence it is written, "there is a friend who is one when the time suits but will not stand by in your day of trouble." Remove his hope of reward, and at once, he ceases to be your friend. Someone has satirized such friendship in a neat verse: One who comes in good fortune and goes in misfortune loves not the person but the person's purse. The beginning of this perverted friendship, however, often entices people to share true friendship. Those who first make a pact in the hope of common gain reach a summit of pleasurable agreement, if only in human affairs, as long as they remain true to themselves with this mammon of iniquity. In no way, however, should this be called a genuine friendship, for it begins and continues in the hope of temporal gain.

Spiritual Friendship

Now the spiritual, which we call true friendship, is desired not with an eye to any worldly profit or for any extraneous reason, but for its own natural worth and for the emotion of the human heart so that its fruit and reward is nothing but itself. So spiritual friendship is begotten among the righteous by the likeness of life, habits, and interests, that is, by agreement in things human and divine, with goodwill and charity. Now I think this definition adequately expresses friendship, provided that by our mention of charity, as is our habit, we mean to exclude every vice from friendship and provided that by goodwill, we mean the delightful awakening within us. Where such friendship exists, wishing and not wishing the same things, a wish that is the more pleasant as it is more sincere and the sweeter as it is more holy and can wish for nothing that is unbecoming and fail to wish for nothing that is becoming. Of course, prudence guides, justice rules, strength protects, and temperance moderates this friendship.[6]

To Aelred of Rievaulx, we would like to provide a quantitative and qualitative diagram of what we feel is a more current description of the types of friendships:

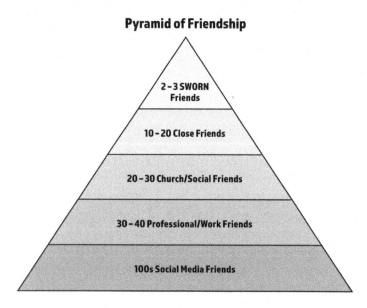

Pyramid of Friendship

2 – 3 SWORN Friends

10 – 20 Close Friends

20 – 30 Church/Social Friends

30 – 40 Professional/Work Friends

100s Social Media Friends

This is not Aelred's idea, however. He thinks that only spiritual friendship represents a pure form of friendship. Carnal and worldly friendships are not real friendship, although many think they are. In speaking of different kinds of friendship, then, Aelred means to distinguish between true friendship and two different types of false friendship.

In true friendship, the friends are jointly responding to God's call by loving Him and loving their neighbor. These are, to them, the highest goods of human life, and they encourage and sustain each other in answering God's call by pursuing and attaining these goods. Aelred describes friendship based on encouraging each other to love God and neighbor as spiritual friends. We call it "Sworn friendship."

Conditions for Sacred Friendship

And he said, "The kingdom of God is as if a man should scatter seed on the ground. He sleeps and rises night and day, and the seed sprouts and grows; he knows not how. The earth produces by itself, first the blade, then the ear, then the full grain in the ear. But when the grain is ripe, at once, he puts in the sickle, because the harvest has come."

Mark 4: 26-29

C.S. Lewis laments when he observes that for modern man, friendship has become "something quite marginal; not the main course in life's banquette; a diversion; something that fills up the chunks of one's time."

Our hope is that this book can ignite a new commitment to the adventure of friendship, something beyond marginal connection. The parable of the seed growing will help us understand the stages of growth from potential friendship into Sworn friendships. Before friendships sprout certain possible conditions must exist. These conditions are good soil, water, and sunshine. Without these conditions, the seed will fail to germinate, and the hope of something between two men becomes something that never was. Unfortunately, many near occasions of friendship are never realized. Knowing a day without friendship is like a day without honey, we miss out on the underlying sweetness of life. Cicero said, "Virtue is first, but next to it and to it alone, the greatest of all things is friendship."[7]

For a friendship to become Sworn, it needs the six essential ingredients we mentioned previously, but it must get to the Sworn or harvest stage before any of these ingredients begin to have an effect. In order for the stages to begin, the conditions must be present, and so we must be cognizant of these conditions of good soil, water, and sunshine.

Good Soil

First, the soil has to be rich in nutrients for proper germination and growth. In South Florida, when you drive out to Belle Glade, you can see sugar cane fields. The soil there is referred to as "black gold," and it is some sweet dirt for growing crops.

The soil that supports the stages of friendship has to be like "black gold." Initially, there has to be the commitment of time, which leads to exclusivity in friendship. Only so many hours in a day allow for relationship building; therefore, one must make thoughtful decisions about dedicating time to a potential Sworn friendship.

David Horn has written a book entitled *Soul Mates*. In the book, he articulates several conditions for friendship. First, he says friendship is exclusive. It is enjoyed by a few because we don't have time for more than a few. You can't overcrowd the soil by attempting to plant seeds on top of each other. Friendship is for a few and is limited by location or proximity. We do "life together." The soil of exclusivity produces friendship in close proximity when circumstance allows for it.

Horn speaks of friendship as preferential, another soil condition. In order for friendship to be of high quality, it has to be preferred. For it to be preferred, it has to be worked at exclusively. True friendship is rare and highly selective.

Immanuel Kant insists, "Is every man a possible friend for us? No. I can be a friend of mankind in general in the sense that I can bear good-will in my heart toward everyone, but to be the friend of everybody is impossible, for friendship is a particular relationship, and he who is a friend to everyone has not a particular friend."[8]

We run the risk of cheapening true friendships by having too many friends. In social situations, it is necessary to "be friendly," but it doesn't mean we become friends with everyone we meet. Friendship is work, and we must till the soil of preferred friendship with a commitment to work at it. Timely communication—as we found out on many interviews during our Philadelphia mancation (Chapter VII)—is evidence of preferential treatment. Effective communication is work. We "work" the soil so that a potential friendship has a chance to grow.

The fruit of sacred friendship is a rare melding of souls. Augustine refers to a friend as a "second self."[9] The loss of his friend produced an incredible ache deep within, a never-ending sorrow. (Eric Nielson has helped me more than anyone to understand this incredible ache when he speaks about his Sworn friend, Stephen Pitcairn, who died tragically... never forgotten.) Augustine experienced a sharing of identities, but this was only able to occur because he preferred this one friend over many and therefore gained a true, Sworn friend.

Water

A second condition for potential friendship to become Sworn is water. The water of friendship is reciprocity. Friendship must be reciprocal, as we have mentioned before. Some requests for friendship cannot be reciprocated. If Peter wasn't interested in befriending me, it could become awkward and slip into pathological obsession if I pursued something he didn't want. Movies have been made about unreciprocated attractions that get weird. Friendship is not a one-way street. The rain must fall on both for it to have a chance.

In addition, rain falls on friendship because there is a perceived benefit. Friendship is selfish in some ways. By nature, one must believe that something is received from a friend. Friendship is self-benefiting. It's a two-way street. A perceived leech of life is avoided. Friends must come with benefits. What is gained by Sworn friendship that is different from the quid pro quo type of friendship? What is achieved is spirit and love. Friendship for friendship's sake is incredibly life-giving. It truly is beneficial and is highly valued and sought after because the benefit sweetens life like a bowl full of honey. Sometimes friends "do nothing together, which often leads to the very best something," a much-loved quote from Winnie-the-Pooh who had a Sworn friend in Christopher Robin.

Sun

A third condition for potential friendship to become a Sworn friendship is the warmth that comes from the sun. For the sun to shine on friendship, it has to be freely chosen. There can be no obligations or hidden motives. C.S. Lewis says, "Hence the exquisite arbitrariness and irresponsibility of this love. I have no duty to be one's friend, and no man in the world has a duty to be mine. No claims, no shadow of necessity, friendship is unnecessary, like philosophy, like art, like the universe itself (for God did not need to create). It has no survival value; rather, it is one of those things which give value to survival."[10]

The seeds of friendship sense the sun's warmth when friendship is an end in itself. We must hold this friendship lightly with no pressure or demands. Advice given, but not heeded, doesn't threaten this kind of friendship.

Finally, friendship is dynamic. Just as the sun moves across the sky, friendship is always changing. It's in flux. It advances and retreats. It is fragile and vulnerable. Peter may suggest to me, "If we are friends, prove it." Our friendship could grow, or it could die, becoming a failed friendship. Aelred of Rievaulx says that if a friendship can end, then it never was. There may be some truth to that, but it's not the entire story. If not cared for, it can wither and die. Like my basil plants I forgot to water, they are no longer with us. Friendship must stand the test of time, and when found worthy must be nurtured dynamically or may be scorched by the sun and wither.

Stages of Sacred Friendship

As we reflected on the conditions necessary for friendship's growth with the parable of the growing seed as a backdrop, now we hope to contemplate stages of growth with the same parable. The Kingdom of God grows when friendship is valued as the pearl of great price. When it is sought after and cherished, like a friendship founded on loyalty, as Bobby, our Uber driver stated, "I wouldn't sell my friend out for a million dollars… that's what loyalty is…" The kingdom of friendship increases when men commit to being open to more profound experiences of friendship.

In the parable, a man scatters seed on the ground. He then patiently waits as the seed sprouts. The seed sheds its outer shell of the false self with its commitment to selfish, self-absorbed, and self-sabotaging patterns of relating to one self and those around us. The seed must die for it to live. We must awake from our slumber and embrace a journey of growing self-awareness. The seed must begin the journey to fruitfulness. This growth is a mystery, for friendship itself is a mysterious journey. The earth, in the parable, produces by itself, and the farmer knows not how, but simply allows the process to take place in time, shrouded in contemplation. Then the blade emerges, then the ear, then the full grain in the ear, and later it ripens for the harvest.

The stages of the growth for the seed are transferable to the stages of growth for friendship. In the spiritual journey, a person typically progresses through five thresholds. (I am indebted to Don Everts and Doug Schaupp for their discovery of the five thresholds they write about in *I Once Was Lost.*)

First, one must trust another further along the spiritual path. Second, trust leads to curiosity as it relates to spiritual inquiry. Third, curiosity leads to lifestyle change in which decisions are made in order to deepen one's awareness of God and self. Fourth, meandering leads to seeking as the sojourner is more intentional and purposeful in their spiritual pursuits. Fifth, finally, a mysterious, wonderful, and organic ripening occurs, placing the person in a state of union with God. We can refer to this experience as being "born again," waking up, accepting Christ, or being seized with the power of great affection.

However we choose to speak about it is important, but not as important as the new way of being with God, self, and others. When we wake up, we see the world through a new lens. We know the world through the Creator's eyes, the eyes of love and life. We are all created in His image and likeness; therefore, I will never meet a person that doesn't deserve my love and acceptance. This spiritual awakening Peter and I have both experienced. We believe it is the true foundation and cornerstone of Sworn friendship.

In about an hour, "Suds' buds" are leaving Starbucks and heading to the Monk's Café in Philly, where they will be unveiling and tapping a friendship brew. Apparently, a special once-a-year beer is also being simultaneously tapped at 3:00PM all around the world. We walked past the Monk Café this morning on the way to get a straight-edge shave at Dukes Barber Shop and noticed about 20 folks camping out awaiting the unveiling. After chatting with Jeff and interviewing him (see interview link and image in Chapter VII), he heard my name was Suds and said, "Cool suds and buds," and so the phrase was coined.

Sorry, back to stages. As we reflect on the stages of our friendship, we want to compare it to the growth of a vineyard, from seed to ripened fruit. First, the seed must fall to the ground. The seed of friendship is scattered when two men meet for the first time and experience a positive first impression. It can begin for several reasons and under various circumstances, but first impressions matter. Without a good first impression, progressing through the stages of friendship is likely dead in the H^2O.

When I first met Peter, he was with PBA President Bill Fleming, who I respected, and he was always intentional, so I knew that he thought that Peter and I had a chance to become buds. Peter was a lax-bro, so he knew there was a connection. That encounter led to a bro-date for breakfast.

The seedling of our friendship emerged over the course of several deliberate occasions. During that time, we both realized independently that the friendship was worth pursuing. The small plant grew into a vine. As we began to do life together, we spent time with our sons, playing lacrosse, fishing trips to Montana, sharing laughter and tears as we grew to know each other better. Stage four, the fruit of our friendship, appeared. It took the form of us serving together on mission trips to the Dominican Republic. We served as Board Members of FCA – Lacrosse program, as well as mentoring PBA lacrosse players. Our commitment to altruism, which is a distinct element of our definition of friendship, is evidence of our desire to be on mission together. We affectionately referred to this as bromission. Finally, the ripened fruit led to the harvest of our Sworn friendship. Peter and I cut a covenant of commitment to our six ingredients of sacred friendship, which are again: Friendship with God, Common Interests, Loyalty, Vulnerability, Equality, and Self-Awareness.

Finally, a thought from Aelred:

> What statement about friendship can be more sublime, more true, and more valuable than this: it has been proved that friendship must begin in Christ, continue with Christ, and be perfected by Christ.

Aelred[11]

Chapter IV
Manaffection

Should we keep kissing our sons?

And as soon as the boy had gone, David rose
from beside the ground and bowed three times.
And they kissed one another and wept with one
another, David weeping the most.

I Samuel 40:41

Manaffection doesn't mean that two dudes should sit on the same side of the booth at breakfast, although that could be an interesting experiment, but too each his own. And manaffection doesn't necessarily mean three guys should sit in the front seat of a pickup truck together when going shooting, but again, whatever floats your boat.

Please feel free to send us your manaffection photos. Scratch that, Peter just said he's not interested in your front seat selfies.

In our opinion, manaffection is the ability of a man to freely express his affection to a friend, son, or daughter. We believe our society is beginning to warm up to the idea that men, by necessity, need to express affection to loved ones. But there are still those that shy away from the expression of physical affection for various reasons, and that's cool.

Quick story...

So there's this guy who went on a youth a mission trip with me (Suds) years ago. He liked to give surprise back rubs. Let's affectionately call him Back Rub Guy or "BRG" for short. BRG was six foot two inches and 230 pounds=a big dude. His heart was as big as his body, and he would give surprise back rubs to guys on the mission trip. No big deal? Most of the guys on that mission trip were on my high school lacrosse team, and I could tell by the way they squirmed that they were not pleased with BRG's innocent massage therapy… rejecting his manaffection. It eventually came to a tipping point on the third day when I was approached by several of the guys. "Please tell Doug to stop touching us. Doug is a nice enough guy, but we can't handle his surprise massages. It's creeping us out."

So, I had to approach BRG and suggest that although he was personally comfortable with this way of expressing affection these guys were threatening me with mutiny. So I asked him to refrain from this form of manaffection.

Fast forward to the end of the trip after the guys got to know BRG, their hearts had softened up, and muscles were sore. They actually openly admitted missing BRG's surprise massages.

Note to self: physical affection is not a bad thing, but actually a much-needed form of expression by many men. It's the way we were created, period, end of the story.

When we hugged and kissed our sons when they were little, Peter and I, whether we realized it or not, were giving our sons what they needed as they matured from being small boys to younger men. We're not really overly affectionate guys. Manaffection is forced at times. Still, we know when we hug our sons that we are delivering to their souls something that only a father can give. We impart a sense of worth and an understanding that they are cherished. Never would we say that this softens them in any way, but we know many men that would say and have actually said that it softens your sons to hug and kiss them.

Another quick story...

My (Suds') first son, Joshua, was born with a myriad of complications that restricted him to a wheelchair. My wife and I traveled with Joshua from Boston to visit friends in South Carolina. When visiting one of my buddies, who was a football coach, I leaned down and kissed Joshua on the forehead. My buddy immediately chastised me for kissing him, suggesting I would make Joshua soft by kissing him. So in Suds fashion, I kissed him again.

Physical affection, as many studies have shown, provides life. Small infants that are not held in nurseries fail to thrive. Again, we are created with this need. It does not stop at 10 pounds, 50 pounds, 100 pounds, or 200 pounds. Unfortunately, it seems to us that society feels after a certain age men should not hug one another. When I hug a friend I'm expressing to him I care in a way that a simple handshake doesn't accomplish. To be clear, we don't hug guys we meet for the first time. No hugging on the first bro-date. (In the wake of COVID-19, handshakes and hugs may be gone forever, so perhaps a fist-pump will be the new norm but we're hoping not.)

Manaffection (we know some of you still cringe when you say it) grows in an open-hearted and safe environment.

Who knows, maybe we'll see it in Webster's Dictionary at some point. Until then, don't stop hugging your sons.

One more quick story…

So, Suds has these "Man Gatherings" at his house once a month. I (Peter) affectionately call them "Friday Night Sausage Fests." Anyway, I digress. At one of the Friday Night Bromie Gatherings—after the charcuterie board of cheese and meat, escargot and oysters, but before the chubby steaks with bacon-wrapped asparagus and post-dinner cigars… I digress again. (Suds does throw a mean Bromie Gathering and he's a good cook.) Back to the story. So, I walk out of the kitchen to find Suds in the foyer, looking white as a ghost. I asked him what was wrong, and he replied, "Dale just kissed me."

I asked, "On the lips?"

He said, "No, no, no."

Come to learn that Dale had received a text from his wife that his daughter was at a high school football game where a shooting had just occurred. He had pulled Suds away from the group and explained what had happened and that he had to leave early. With all the emotions Dale was feeling, he instinctively kissed Suds on the cheek in appreciation for his sincere concern for his daughter. This gesture was a pure form of manaffection from one man to another. It was spontaneous from the heart. All was fine with Dale's daughter. In this uncertain world this is a reminder to cherish every moment we get to spend with those we love, especially our sons and daughters. It's more important than ever to express to them a father's love.

WARNING: The section below may have some quoted big words.

Jackson Bliss tells a moving story of affection between men in his October 9, 2018, article entitled "A Scarcity of Affection Among Men:"

> Once, just as I was about to step inside Union Station in New Haven, an old African American guy with fuzzy grey hair and glasses stopped me on the sidewalk and asked me if I had a light. Though technically I'd quit smoking when I'd started grad school, my bad habit resurfaced at the end of every semester because of the stress. It was reading period, so I pulled out my lighter with a little guilt and tried lighting his cigarette. The wind was strong and erratic, though, extinguishing the flame every time I rolled the flint. As I became impatient, I finally grabbed his soft, wilted old hand and cupped it with mine, lighting his cigarette undisturbed. He took a big puff and exhaled. Then he nodded his head, smiled at me, and said: "Thank you, son." By the time I was inside the train station, I was bawling.

Jackson goes on to write:

> The real issue buried underneath my grief was the fact that I rarely got the male affection I'd wanted as a kid. And the sad thing is I'm not the exception either.

We grew up with old school dads that were not very good at expressing themselves. Our dad's hugs were few and far between. Suds recalls a story he's never forgotten—the time his father embraced him when he suffered a Little League Baseball loss. He was the first one to meet Suds when he walked off the field. He remembers his father embracing him, telling him he loved him. That moment is seared in his memory for eternity. Unlike Suds, I can't remember my father showing me physical affection, but I can remember his presence and offering his wisdom in times of need.

Jackson continues to write:

> One of the pernicious consequences of living in a country still struggling with homophobia, social verticality, and patriarchy is not just the rigid gender roles this system imposes on men (and obviously women), but also the way it prevents grown men from expressing love, gratitude and affection to each other (and often to their sons). Because of this, many boys grow up seeing affection as inherently unmasculine because their fathers never modeled affection and unconditional love as a constituent part of their own masculinity.

We wholeheartedly agree that the ongoing poverty of male affection in our society has harmed all of us, especially our boys. Jackson writes:

> Boys grow up seeing affection as sexual behavior and not social behavior.

We believe that there is this void within ourselves and have often seen it in other men. This emotional vacuum stifles men from expressing social affection, not to be confused with social distancing. We write this book to address a need, a need for men to permit themselves to feel and physically express themselves to those they love. Sworn friendship is an essential way to call forth this form of expression hidden in men's wounded souls.

One last quick story...

It happened without warning. I should have remembered, but I blanked on this one. The man kiss was culturally acceptable and embraced by this side of my family, but I had forgotten. As I greeted my cousin's husband, he, without hesitation, hugged me and kissed me on the cheek. I felt my butt cheeks clench as I experienced this unfamiliar expression of manaffection.

We sat down for pizza (New York pizza is ridiculous) and had a great time catching up. Then it happened again. You would think I would have been prepared, but I wasn't. Charles, Chuck's son, arrived home after work, and without warning, he planted one on my cheek when I jumped up to greet him. I froze up like an icicle, and it was July. It must have been obvious because the entire family was laughing.

The next day my wife, my kids, and I were heading from Long Island to NYC for a little sightseeing adventure. We parked our car at the train station, where David's Taxi has a parking lot. Charles showed me where to park the car. And I guess you can say, three times is a charm or three strikes you're out. It happened. He kissed me again. But this time, I was ready, and I sincerely appreciated the tenderness of a kiss from someone who wasn't afraid to express his love for his family.

Three months later, Charles died unexpectedly. This chapter is dedicated to him. Charles helped me understand the importance of physical affection. Rest in peace, little brother. We love you very much...

Chapter V
Mantimacy
('man-in-me-see')

Don't be scared, it's weird.

Reedism #8

You can say it. This is kinda weird. This is a risky play on words, and some of you might be cringing again, but we believe to live without risk is to risk not living. Authentic manhood demands that we live open-hearted, granting ourselves permission to feel and express that feeling to other men. Vulnerability, a key ingredient of sacred friendship, is essential on our journey to authentic manhood. We men excel in our ability to figure things out in our minds. We have been conditioned to live "externally" as we address family dynamics and workplace challenges.

As men, we fix things. We fix with our words. We fix with our hands. We fix with our strategic plans, and unfortunately, we men at times fix by shaming those closest to us. Not our best moments, but we men often forget to fix ourselves. We don't allow ourselves to express true feelings. We have them packed away in the emotional lockers of our souls. Of course, we can't trust our emotions. They slow us down and soften us. We can't slow down, we can't be soft. Marshmallow Men don't make it. It's go time! Game on! Dudes check their hankies at the door.

That's all rubbish.

Authentic men feel. Sacred friendship demands, elicits, encourages the other friend to pay attention to and become more aware of their hearts, thereby living more open-hearted lives.

The timely text exchange between Suds and me below is an example of me, Peter, being authentic and sharing my feelings with Suds.

Peter 1/24/19 – 5:37PM:

Was reading some of my old Sworn notes and thought I would share this one with you, my Sworn Friend… "I admire Suds for his ability to connect with so many… it's a true gift/blessing. I'm honored when he calls me his sworn friend. Maybe I didn't do the best as husband or a father, but perhaps God is allowing me to get right with this friendship…"

Suds 1/24/19 – 5:56PM (his heartfelt response):

Dude… that was solid mantimacy… love you too, brother!!

So you ask: what is the value of the mantimacy? Great question. We have no idea. We needed another chapter and wanted to see if the word "mantimacy" would get picked up by Webster's Dictionary.

In all honesty, we run the risk of living a two-thirds existence if we neglect sharing our hearts. We as men live in our minds and react with our guts while emotions remain packed away. But authentic manhood is being fully alive, living completely with open minds, hearts, and guts. To truly experience Sworn friendship, men must allow their hearts to knit together. David and Jonathan experienced this type of Sworn friendship. It was holy ground.

> When he had finished speaking to Saul, the soul of Jonathan was knit to the soul of David, and Jonathan loved him as his own soul.

I Samuel 18:1

The biblical word "soul" is synonymous with heart. Jonathan and David experienced a gift from God, one we all long for, whether we know it or not. The One who created us longs for our hearts to knit with His, and in turn, we become able to knit our hearts in friendship with men. So our friendship with God leads to the opportunity of friendship with another man. We are wired for this type of social interaction, which leads to the emotional tying of one man's heart to another man's. We work best when we are on mission with another brother… sharing laughter, tears, joy, sorrow, and an occasional Twisted Trunk IPGA. (Luv you, Reiny… thanks for creating a safe space that has allowed us to develop friendships.)

I'm growing in my love for Peter.

I'm growing in my love for Suds.

There are no "I dos" here, but there is absolutely a commitment until death do us part, in richness and in health…

My love for Peter deepens as we do life together. I look forward to spending time with my Sworn friend. The writing of this book has been a blast, but also a gift as my soul has expanded. I feel more fully alive because I have a soul friend like Peter. He loves with his time, advice, laughter, and an occasional awkward, but authentic manaffection moment. My life would be less complete without him. One day he or I shall pass. Obviously, not sure who will go first, but I'm confident that if it was me, he would share at my funeral as David did for Jonathan. He would honor me and do everything in his power to care for my family. While I don't have plans on checking out any time soon, knowing I have a sacred friend/brother like Peter is comforting all the more. Enough of the mantimacy stuff, but as Peter is quick to say, "Life without friendship would not be complete."

We have identified key ingredients of sacred friendship in Chapter II. We strongly feel that for two friends to develop a deepening intimacy, which we refer to as mantimacy and Deuteronomy 13:7 refers to as a friend "who is your own soul," there are two non-negotiables: trust and vulnerability.

Man-Trust

What does it mean? What does it look like? We struggle with this probably because life is tough. After half a century on this planet, you accumulate a lot of emotional wounds, many of which have eroded trust in mankind. Inner-work is necessary to heal these aged emotional wounds. Emotional rehabilitation takes place when you decide to trust another individual, in this case another man, with intimate feelings. As we did when we met years ago, we continue today to work willingly and intentionally at sharing our feelings. Man-trust happens when two guys don't check their hankies at the door and are comfortable enough to share a few tears. That's what we believe man-trust looks like.

Man-Vulnerability

We'll make this one quick, but it's not easy for dudes. Simply put, it's a soul spill—one friend spilling their soul to another.

We feel that Sirach 6:14-16 captures this: "A faithful friend is a sturdy shelter: he that has found one has found a treasure. There is nothing as precious as a faithful friend, and no scales can measure his excellence." Also: "A faithful friend is an elixir of life, and those who fear the Lord will find him." These verses describe the result of heartfelt Sworn friendship filled with trust and vulnerability. It is a "sturdy shelter, a treasure, and elixir of life." Those who have a friendship with God will find this Sworn friend.

Fermented Friendship

Forsake not an old friend, for a new one does not compare with him. A new friend is like new wine; when it has aged, you will drink it with pleasure.

Sirach 9:14-15

We have definitely experienced this kind of friendship we refer to as "fermented." On the way to our writing man cave, which doubles as the library for the church, we were joking on how long we've been at this writing project... three years and counting. There you go, fermentation, bromie.

Sworn friendship doesn't happen overnight. It ages, matures, deepens, it ferments. Like a fine wine, it just gets better with age. I razz Suds about how long it's taken to write the book, but to be honest, this book would not be the book it is if we written it in a month or two. The experience of writing this book and the time we have spent together has fermented our friendship. The writing sessions, sometimes at the North Palm monastery, church library, plane rides, minivan, or random restaurants, are times I look forward to. As we approach the end, I find myself wondering, "What's next?"

A quick story…

Another close, sacred friend is my buddy Paul. His friendship has invited and encouraged me to become more open-hearted. We became acquainted when I was the Head Men's Lacrosse Coach at Palm Beach Atlantic University, and his son Fritz played for me (no longer a player but now a true Sworn friend). Paul had been burned by clergy years before, so naturally, he was cautious. I didn't blame him. Broken trust is a serious thing. I'm a wee bit over the top when you first meet me, loud and energetic, but definitely sincere and welcoming.

Our friendship matured over the coming months that led to years over weekly breakfasts at Testa's restaurant and lunches at The Tiki-Hut. Both establishments have subsequently closed, but our friendship remains. Paul always brought the gift of vulnerability, and our man-trust grew. I experienced a growing intimacy with my friend that enabled me to weather many storms and transitions. Paul became a firm foundation.

One of my fondest memories was a mission trip that Paul and I took to the Dominican Republic with several PBA lacrosse players. On that trip, we built a house for a Haitian woman named Estreya and her family. She had lost her husband and was living with her small children in a hut pieced together with scraps of wood and sheet metal. The shared experience of two friends on a mission was priceless. When we handed her keys to her new home for the first time, I turned and noticed tears streaming down Paul's face. I asked if he was okay. He simply responded that this was the purest thing he's ever done. Vulnerability gives birth to vulnerability. Trust gives way to trust. Intimacy grows in the soil of both. My friendship with Paul has and always will be a sacred journey of open-hearted intimacy.

One last story...

Paul and I share a love for a personality theory called the "enneagram." (More about the enneagram in the next book.) We attended an enneagram conference in Montreat, North Carolina. One night we visited Mt. Pisgah Brewery. It was there that I came to understand that when it comes to beer brewing Germans were technicians, but Belgium brewers were artists. (Reiny, you will always be our favorite technician. Shout out for Palm Beach Pils.)

Paul and I grabbed a beer and made our way over to the fire pit. Two bromies on a man-date engaged Paul and me in conversation. When we shared that we were attending a psych conference, they immediately assumed we were licensed psychotherapists. In reality, we both needed deep psycho-therapy ourselves. Our new found fire pit friends

John 15:12-17

This is my commandment that you love one another as I have loved you. **Greater love has no one than this that someone lay down his life for his friends. You are my friends** if you do what I command you. No longer do I call you servants, for the servant does not know what his master is doing; but I have called you **friends**, for all that I have heard from my Father I have made known to you. You did not choose me, but I chose you and appointed you that you should go and bear fruit and that your fruit should abide, so that whatever you ask the Father in my name, he may give it to you. These things I command you so that you will love one another.

John 15:12-17

If we're wondering what love might look like in the context of a Sworn friendship, Jesus tells us, "My commandment is this: that you love one another as I have loved you," (John 15:12). He goes on to drive the point home by saying, "No greater love exists than this… that someone lay down his life for his friends." That is precisely what Jesus did. The cross was evidence of friendship. Jesus' ministry is grounded in God's suffering love and solidarity with the human condition. Jesus knows what it's like to be one of us. He experienced what it was like to be born, to live, and to die. Dietrich Bonhoeffer, the great German Theologian and author of *The Cost of*

Discipleship said, in the face of his own suffering, "Only the Suffering God can help."

In the time Jesus walked on earth, "friendships supreme duty may have involved self-sacrifice for one's friend, even to the point of death."[1] This friendship associated with the cross had its conditions. Jesus referred to those as friends who did what He asked them to do. Friendship with Jesus is elevated beyond the designation of a disciple. It is a mature, loyal, and reliable relationship. Sworn friends understand the potential cost associated with this depth of friendship. Therefore, it is highly valued and not to be taken lightly. The demand associated with it, based on Jesus' pronouncement, may require an ultimate sacrifice.

Brennan Manning, a Catholic Priest who has written extensively about the grace of God he has received at the foot of the cross, tells a story about a foxhole friend. I can't remember all the details, but it goes something like this:

Two friends were in a foxhole when a hand grenade was thrown in the middle, one friend dove on top of the grenade saving the other friend... When home after the war, the one friend wondered out loud about his friend's love for him, the one who jumped on the grenade. Overhearing the statement, the friends' mother exclaimed, "My god, how much did he love you, he died for you!"

As Jesus said, "Greater love has no one than this that he lay down his life for his friend(s)."

The status of friendship with Jesus comes with expectations. This relationship is not a right but a privilege. With it comes the responsibility of bearing fruit while being on mission. Jesus gives his friends a mission. The company of Jesus was enjoyed and savored by those who took this mission seriously. The idle rarely lasted as friends of Jesus because their idleness was evidence that they lacked understanding and therefore lacked the ability to be friends. I guess you could call them "fair-weather friends." Cross-bearing was not something they signed up for, and cross-bearing was part of the gig. Friends of Jesus increasingly came to understand what this friendship cost and it was not cheap.

Who are Jesus' friends? That's a critical question for all of us to wrestle with. Friendship is a choice. Jesus doesn't have to be our friend, but our obedience makes that a possibility. By calling his disciples friends, Jesus is characterizing them in a more intimate way. Again, the relationship is elevated to a more heartfelt commitment. A desire to please Jesus emerges in the hearts of his close followers now referred to as friends. Jesus' friends are given an increased knowledge of what the Father is doing. This knowledge gives birth to greater joy in the relationship. Obedience becomes less burdensome.

The kind of friendship Jesus is talking about is one that inspires mission. The mission to proclaim the kingdom of God. As we defined friendship earlier, "Sworn friendship can be defined as a reciprocal freely agreed upon guardianship of one another's soul with the purpose of unity of spirit, commitment to mission, and shared growth in the sacred journey of friendship with God." This friendship desires to leave the world better than we found it. The kind of love that requires one to give his life for a friend is the kind of love that explodes into a shared mission to a suffering world with the suffering love of the Savior.

Mark 15:21-22

And they compelled a passerby, Simon of Cyrene, who was coming in from the country, the father of Alexander and Rufus, to carry his cross. And they brought him to the place called Golgotha (which means Place of a Skull).

Mark 15:21-22

The victim of crucifixion was normally forced to carry his own cross from within the city to the place of crucifixion outside the city. Probably due to weakness, Jesus was not able to carry his cross all the way.

Robert H. Stein, author of Mark[2]

The suffering love of God, displayed in His walk to Golgotha, is a redemptive act but also an invitation to suffer with Him. Imagine Jesus talking to Simon of Cyrene, "I've come to suffer with you so suffer with me." Simon was pressed into service. Where were Jesus' friends? They were nowhere to be found. Sometimes this road must be walked alone, but it doesn't have to be lonely. Even though Jesus' closest friends exhibited fickleness and weak loyalty, a stranger befriended Jesus for a brief time during an especially difficult moment in Jesus' journey to Golgotha. We have or most likely will experience this aspect of the journey. Sworn friends at this point are not "unSworn." It's just that this form of suffering is often experienced apart from those closest to you.

However, God may send a stranger who appears with perfect timing during the weakest moments of our lives. For this brief time span, they are absolutely the embodiment of a Sworn, soul loving friend, like Simon was to Jesus. To be clear, Simon was not a willing cross-bearer, but as often is true, neither are we. We are not called to look for suffering, but we are called to cross bear for others even when it's not convenient or desirable.

A deepening understanding of cross-bearing for Sworn friends leads to deepening love and solidarity for the friend, which leads to deepening love and solidarity for all humanity. Sworn friends share pain, failure, and anguish. It's okay to feel hurt over broken dreams and relationships.

Sworn friends encourage the other to speak about their pain, to acknowledge, accept, and articulate it. For what remains in the dark has power over us.

> The cross is the great Christian answer to the world as a problem. The cross is liberation. The cross is the only liberation from servitude to the illusions which are packaged and sold as the world. The cross transforms the world, and once the cross has been accepted fully in our life then we can begin to make sense about the whole entity, the world.
>
> **James Finley**[3]

Simon accepted the cross and journeyed with his new friend to Golgotha. Our hope is that men everywhere embrace the joy that ultimately comes with walking through suffering, with a Sworn friend. At the foot of the cross, sacred friendship gains all by losing all. We gain a humility that deepens our love for God, ourselves, and others.

> In prayer, we hang upon the cross with the thief at Christ's right side. As Christ hangs dying, we hear Him tell us… "this day, you will be with Me in paradise."
>
> **James Finley**[4]

And it's not the Paradise Island reality show on ABC. I remember fondly the one night when Peter and I spent an hour in prayer at the chapel in the Passionate Monastery in North Palm Beach. As we prayed, it was evident that we knelt with Christ between us. Like the two thieves on either side of the cross, we struggled in prayer to trust Christ as he invited us to enter paradise with Him. Prayer is foundational for the friendship we call "Sworn" because, as our thoughts above express: in prayer, we understand what it means to die to those things which are meaningless and live for what matters most: our friendship with God, our friendship with ourselves, and our friendship with a chosen few.

> Suddenly, in the midst of all our thievery and pain, Christ's cross becomes our own, and we discover that His death becomes our life.
>
> **James Finley**[5]

As thieves, scammers and manipulators, deceptive and cunning, full of pain, Sworn friends seek transformative death. As sojourners, we keep an eye on the prize of the upward calling of union with God with the sole purpose of finding what matters most, a peace that promises us that "all shall be well, and all shall be well, and all manner of thing shall be well" (Julian of Norwich).

Two Dimensions of the Cross for Deepening Sworn Friendship

1. **Vertical** – a root awareness and longing for divine presence, a deep desire to experience transcendence offered to us in Christ.

2. **Horizontal** – we do not journey to God in isolation, but with those closest to us, our Sworn friends.

The paradox of the cross is that the horizontal and vertical dimensions of our spiritual journey meet and become one. A man fully alive is one full of love for God and others. Unfortunately, we come face to face with our selfish, narcissistic selves full of excuses why we need to look out for #1, and off we go further into the grey city spoken of by C.S. Lewis in *The Great Divorce*. We divorce ourselves from God and others until we are "happily" alone in our little existence. We believe it is an abundant life, but it's a lie. A lie we hopefully wake from and discover the light coming into the darkness of our deceit.

In cross bearing friendships we choose to love as Christ did, willing to be a living sacrifice so that love might be birthed within us. Again, the cross changes everything. We increase in wisdom and stature with God and man. Sworn friends understand the magnitude of this relationship forged at the foot of the cross. It changes everything. We are unable to live solely for ourselves, but we sense growing solidarity with the poor and forgotten. Sworn friends ignite this desire for mission within one another. In the face of suffering, pain, and brokenness, spiritual friends help each other live honestly. They set out together on a mission to remind those encountered along the way that the Father will always have the last word.

Luke 9:22-23

> The Son of Man must suffer many things and be rejected by the elders, the chief priests and the teachers of the law, and he must be killed and on the third day be raised to life. Then he said to them all: "Whoever wants to be my disciple must deny themselves and take up their cross daily and follow me."

Luke 9:22-23

The Way is the Way of the cross. Followers or friends of Jesus increasingly understand as they experience life that suffering cannot be avoided. Still, it is to be embraced knowing that to be a true disciple is to be a cross-bearer. We are invited to deny ourselves by rejecting the lies offered by a world committed to security and comfort. The comfort and security we write about is the kind that chooses not to notice the suffering of others. Sworn friendship helps the other acknowledge and own the brokenness of this world. This friendship reminds us that suffering is real and that Christ enters this suffering by way of Calvary. The cross is not to be despised, but picked up and carried to wherever the suffering Messiah would ask us to carry it.

Douglas John Hall in his book, *The Cross in Our Context*, recalls a story:

> According to the oral tradition, Peter, "the rock" (Matthew 16:18), the reputed cornerstone of Christ's church, in a manner entirely consistent with his behavior as it is recorded in the Gospels is in the act of fleeing Rome, where many Christians are undergoing the horrors of mad Nero's persecution. The old fisherman is moving with all possible haste along the Appian Way, lined with tombs of patrician Romans, when suddenly he is approached by a vision of the Christ himself, heading in the opposite direction. "Quo Vadis, Domine?" "Where are you going, Lord?" he asks. And the vision answers: "Into Rome, to be crucified again." Then Peter, once more humbled by truth, turns about and makes his way back into the flaming city and – according to tradition – to his own upside down crucifixion.

Douglas John Hall[6]

Sworn friends are brothers in arms—foxhole friends. In the movie *Backdraft*, a moving film about friendship and brotherhood, the sworn oath of firemen is, "If you go, we go." Unless we dare to face the storms, when possible, with our Sworn friend and if necessary alone (although we are never really alone), we will never truly experience the costly grace exhibited on the cross. The cross has to be the center of any true Sacred Friendship. Brothers in arms journey together to the place of the skull, Golgotha, in order to die so that we may live. For daily, we die. Emanuel, God with us, is the suffering God. He is the crucified God. Some say Jesus suffered and God had compassion. Compassion as we understand it is "suffering with." God loves because He suffers. Sworn friends "suffer with" one another. They love because they suffer. Peter and I pick up our crosses daily because we are asked to by the one who bore *the* cross for the salvation of the world.

In America, we are plagued with the inability to suffer. Our experiences have led us to assert that a Sworn friend becomes sacred when friends encourage each other to enter into the pain of this world. We are motivated to live in the shadow of death where His rod and staff comfort us. Life is always more mysterious than our theories about life; therefore, true friendship embraces the mystery and anticipates the unmanageable.

The bond Peter and I have is "in the blood" (to quote my friend Jeremiah Jones), and the bond is always made at the foot of the cross. Sworn friendship is not for the fragile. We must develop a stomach for suffering. Just because we theorize pain out of existence doesn't mean it ceases to exist. Repressed suffering must be paid for by those in proximity to it. Suffering will pay us all a visit in some form, at some time, and there is no panacea, no quick fix, only the presence of friends, human and divine.

The Cross, Crisis, and Companions along the Way

Not too many days into the coronavirus crisis, I experienced a deep sense of dread. It was strange. I'd never experienced anything like it before. I felt overwhelmed by a sense of uncertainty (as did many). I questioned my self-worth. I questioned my identity. We wrote earlier about FEAR or False Events Appearing Real. I think this was that type of fear. It's not that the virus wasn't real, but rather my internal reaction to the crisis seemed manufactured by something outside myself. The fear did not seem to come from within me but from outside of me.

I felt accused, deceived, and I guess you could say psychologically tormented. I came to find out that others were experiencing something similar. I shared with my wife what felt like a paralysis of my soul. She tenderly asked if she could pray for me. Without hesitation I responded, "Would you please?" In that moment I experienced a lifting of what felt like darkness. Prayer has a way of bringing clarity to uncertainty. My wife reminded me that I belong to God and that God was my friend.

Friendship in the midst of crisis is crucial. I also shared my experience with Peter who reminded me who I was. He also reminded me how God had used me in the lives of many, including his own. The encouraging words of a friend have the ability to change perspective, to light the way in the darkness. Jonah experienced darkness in the belly of the whale. I think now I understand the spiritual darkness associated with being swallowed by forces which traffic in fear. My friendships with brothers like Peter assure me that I don't have to journey alone in this life.

My very good Sworn friend Scott Hansel forwarded me a meditation by Richard Rohr a few days before Easter. We share a love for all things Thomas Merton (a Catholic monk) and have been blessed by the writings of Richard Rohr (a Catholic priest). This morning I read a meditation about suffering. Whenever you read the word "suffering" in Christian writings it's not very long before the author makes a beeline for the cross. (I just realized what a beeline is… We recently started caring for hives of bees in my backyard. The bees definitely have a distinct line they take from the hive in search of life-giving nectar.) I guess you could say our "beeline" brings us life at the foot of the cross. Rohr reflects on the grain that must fall to the ground and die (John 12:24). Often in friendships, we share insights and discoveries that bring life. Bees share flower locations. Friends share our crosses, our suffering, and the life-giving sweetness, the honey, that is produced by that suffering. A grain must fall in order to bring life.

A week into the coronavirus I decided to redo my back lawn. I thought the weed stop I sprayed was actually weed stop but it wasn't. I sprayed total vegetation kill on my grass, which two days later produced what looked like a maze. I was so excited! This was just what I was after... patches of brown, dead grass!

I secured the help of my kiddos and raked the dead grass away in order to plant seed. I always look forward to seeing new life pop out of the ground. The seed breaks and emerges as a blade of grass. Two days passed, then five, then ten, and I saw no evidence of life coming from the seed. I thought of ways to hurt the seed company and store from which I purchased the seed. I could go on Amazon and write a review, perhaps even show a time-lapse video of their failed product. My desire for revenge gave way to a more self-aware response, so I didn't hit send.

Two weeks later, I began to see blades of grass emerging from the soil. Time has a way of changing your perspective. Rohr comments on this in this morning's meditation on suffering, "The genius of Jesus' teaching is that He reveals that God uses tragedy, suffering, pain, betrayal and death itself, not to wound or punish us, but to bring us to a larger identity (John 12:24)."

The shell must first crack for expanded growth. I would have never spent time every morning of holy week with Richard Rohr's meditations if my friend Scott had not sent me that email weeks ago. Friendship, especially in times like these, in the midst of the uncertainty that the coronavirus has produced, is the gift that God has given us all. The hope is that we have the eyes to see this gift when it emerges from the sacred ground of God's suffering love.

> Remember, Red, hope is a good thing, maybe the best of things, and no good thing ever dies. I will be hoping that this letter finds you, and finds you well.
>
> ### *The Shawshank Redemption*

Peter Cordrey, my lacrosse brother and fellow coach, shares an interest in thinking about biblical shepherding as it relates to coaching young men. On a day I needed to hear about hope, he sent me a clip from *The Shawshank Redemption*. Red is reading a letter he found in the field left by Andy Dufresne. In the letter is the quote above about hope. Hope changes everything. Hope sees life where others see death. Hope is a good thing, maybe the best of things. I found this hope in friendship. I have been given hope by the words spoken by my friends. I've shared hope with those whose hope was diminished. It truly may be the best of things. Hope scatters the darkness. Hope shines light.

This hope is sometimes referred to as "mystical hope." It grows in silence (Mark 4). It does not draw attention to itself because to do so would cause our false selves to attempt to control it or redirect it. This hope is a gift of being our true selves in Christ. It emerges in a way we can't truly comprehend, but nevertheless, when we face suffering with courage, this hope grows within. We walk as Jesus did along the Via Delarosa—a very painful walk along dark, uncertain streets. This necessary suffering deepens our self-awareness and releases the gift within, the ability to walk in solidarity with all of humanity in love. This journey is not for the distracted or superficial; rarely do they even consider walking into pain. They prefer to live a cosmetic existence with lies and cover ups. Their number is Legion. But there is hope because this world belongs to the Father of Jesus and He is having His way…

We are hoping you find continued friendship…
companions along the way…

Chapter VII
Philadelphia

This is crazy…

Clark Griswold from *National Lampoons Vacation*

Take a "mancation."

At times, you may need to get outside your normal life and take time to focus on reconnecting with your manliness and your man friends. Mancations are occasions for pure, uninterrupted male bonding. Mancations can be as short as a weekend or as long as a week. The destination can be anywhere, but it should involve manly activities. The best mancation is, of course, camping. Well, maybe not. To be clear, you don't have to be totally roughing it. A lodge in the Montana mountains or retreat house on the beach in Eleuthera works just fine. The great outdoors and a roaring campfire or a sweat lodge are the ideal settings for renewing man friendships. Yes, I did say sweat lodge. Suds fancies himself as part Choctaw Native American Indian, coming from Long Island, NY, so I'm sure you see the connection. He does these sweat lodges every now and then. I've never taken part but heard they're epic. The key to the mancation is to make them an immutable tradition. Set a time and make it an annual happening. You can plan the other things in your life around that non=negotiable date. Check out the Sworn Foundation website at www.SwornFoundation.org for more information on Sworn Man Retreats, led by Suds and Pistol Pete.

Suds and I thought it would be fitting to complete the book *Sworn* with a mancation to Philadelphia (The City of Brotherly Love). That and we know how guys like pictures in their books, so Chapter VII is pretty much all pictures, some of which are videos and if you go to www.SwornFoundation.org or the Sworn Friendship YouTube Channel, you can view some hilarious videos. Suds may actually have a future in video blogs. As for me, I get to carry his selfie stick...

Spirit Flight NK1008 - 26 September 2019...
they let us drive. It's Spirit...

Sam (Reading Terminal – Ambassador)
Faith, Trust, and Loyalty…
key ingredients to a Sworn friendship.

Suds forgot to hit the "on" button for video. Epic miss…

Yo… a mancation to Philly would not be complete without a pic at Rocky statue… Flying high now…

Yes, the City did have this sign painted for us…

Suds, Jackie, & Peter
(Jackie – Server at Serpico Restaurant) provided inspiration
and insight on tattoos, as well as a tasty bourbon drink.

Thought hard about getting matching Sworn tattoos…
decided to wait until the 1,000,000th copy is sold.

Peter trying to secure tickets to the
Phillies vs. Marlins on Vivid Seats.

Suds had to walk me off the ledge before I reached through the phone to strangle the customer service representative. "Just remember, don't let them steal your time/ruin your day..." That was after 45 minutes and several heated exchanges and a few choice words with the customer service rep... That's what friends do: keep you in check when you step over the line. We ultimately got the tickets.

Peter takes Suds to a ball game.
Marlins vs. Phillies – Citizens Bank Park

Marlins 4 – Phillies 5 in 15 innings.
Yes… 15 innings.
Thankful, our kids play(ed) lacrosse…

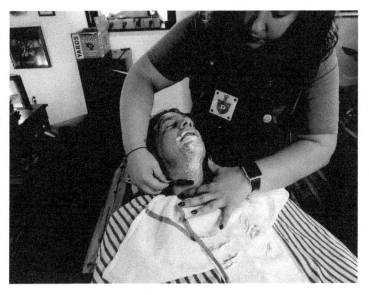

A mancation would not be complete without some pampering. Well, at least Peter feels that way. Reeder is getting a straight edge shave at Dukes Barber Co.

Owen – Dukes Barber Shop – see video #1 with Owen.

Jeff – Monk Café.

Suds and I were able to take part in the tapping of the Belgium Friendship Brew. See video #2 with Jeff.

Loyalty…
"I wouldn't sell out my friend for a million dollars… that's what loyalty is." – Bobby (Uber Driver)

The key ingredients of friendship are …
see video #3 with Luisa

Only in Philly, cheese wiz with your $20s...

Suds at the Air-B&B in South Philly…
A little sketchy, but clean…
Next time: the Four Seasons…

From L-R: Big Brad, Karl the Bee-Keeper, Suds, Reeder, Scooter, and Jonny T at Black Tooth Brewing Co. Sheridan, WY, on the seven brother's trip to Big Horn River, MT, the birthplace of Sworn...

From L-R: Reeder, Big Brad, Suds, and Glynn Miller Band at Tippy's - Eleuthera, Bahamas. Recon trip for Sworn retreat location in Ten Bay, Eleuthera, Bahamas. See video #4 of Big Brad's insightful thoughts on Sworn friendship.

Bibliography

Aelred, et al. *Aelred of Rievaulx: Spiritual Friendship.*
Cistercian Publications, 2010.

Augustine, and Carolyn J.-B. Hammond. *Confessions.*
Harvard University Press, 2014.

Barry, William A. *A Friendship like No Other: Experiencing
God's Amazing Embrace.* Loyola Press, 2008.

Benner, David G. *Sacred Companions: the Gift of Spiritual
Friendship & Direction.* InterVarsity Press, 2004.

Caliguire, Mindy. *Spiritual Friendship.* IVP Connect, 2007.

Finley, James. *Merton's Palace of Nowhere.* Ave Maria Pr,
2018.

Hall, Douglas John. *God & Human Suffering: an Exercise in
the Theology of the Cross.* Ausburg Pub. House,
1986.

Hall, Douglas John. *The Cross in Our Context: Jesus and the
Suffering World.* Fortress Press, 2003.

Horn, David. *Soulmates: Friendship, Fellowship & the
Making of Christian Community.* Hendrickson
Publishers, 2017.

Issler, Klaus Dieter. *Wasting Time with God: a Christian Spirituality of Friendship with God*. InterVarsity Press, 2001.

Kostenberger, Andreas J. *Baker Exegetical Commentary on the New Testament: John*. Baker Academic, 2004.

Leech, Kenneth. *Soul Friend: Spiritual Direction in the Modern World*. Morehouse Pub., 2001.

Lewis, C. S. *The Four Loves*. HarperOne, 2017.

McGinnis, Alan Loy. *The Friendship Factor*. Christian Art, 2008.

McGuire, Brian Patrick. *Friendship and Community: the Monastic Experience, 350-1250: with a New Introduction*. Cornell University Press, 2010.

Meilaender, Gilbert. *Friendship: a Study in Theological Ethics*. University of Notre Dame Press, 1985.

Nehamas, Alexander, and Elisabeth Liebl. *Über Freundschaft*. Dtv Verlagsgesellschaft, 2017.

Olyan, Saul M. *Friendship in the Hebrew Bible*. Yale University Press, 2017.

Pakaluk, Michael. *Other Selves: Philosophers on Friendship*. Hackett, 1991.

Stein, Robert H. *Mark.* Baker Academic, 2010.

Wadell, Paul J. *Becoming Friends: Worship, Justice, and the Practice of Christian Friendship.* Claretian Publications, 2004.

Walsch, Neale Donald. *Friendship with God: an Uncommon Dialogue.* Berkley Books, 2002.

White, Carolinne. *Christian Friendship in the Fourth Century.* Cambridge Univ. Press, 2003.

Willard, Dallas, and Jan Johnson. *Hearing God: Developing a Conversational Relationship with God.* Formatio, 2012.

Wright, Wendy M. *A Retreat with Francis De Sales, Jane De Chantal, and Aelred of Rievaulx: Befriending Each Other in God.* St. Anthony Messenger Press, 1996.

End Notes

CHAPTER II

[1] White, Carolinne. *Christian Friendship in the Fourth Century*. Cambridge Univ. Press, 2003, p.21.

[2] Augustine, and Carolyn J.-B. Hammond. *Confessions*. Harvard University Press, 2014, p.4

[3] Barry, William A. *A Friendship like No Other: Experiencing God's Amazing Embrace*. Loyola Press, 2008, p.8.

[4] Lewis, C. S. *The Four Loves*. Harper One, 2017, p.83

[5] Issler, Klaus Dieter. *Wasting Time with God: a Christian Spirituality of Friendship with God*. InterVarsity Press, 2001, p.52.

[6] Issler, Klaus Dieter. *Wasting Time with God: a Christian Spirituality of Friendship with God*. InterVarsity Press, 2001, p.52

[7] Augustine, and Carolyn J.-B. Hammond. *Confessions*. Harvard University Press, 2014, p.49.

CHAPTER III

[1] Meilaender, Gilbert. *Friendship: a Study in Theological Ethics*. University of Notre Dame Press, 1985, p.1

[2] Meilaender, Gilbert. *Friendship: a Study in Theological Ethics*. University of Notre Dame Press, 1985, p.1

[3] Meilaender, Gilbert. *Friendship: a Study in Theological Ethics*. University of Notre Dame Press, 1985, p.1

[4] Pakaluk, Michael. *Other Selves: Philosophers on Friendship*. Hackett, 1991, p.137.

[5] Pakaluk, Michael. *Other Selves: Philosophers on Friendship*. Hackett, 1991, p.32.

[6] Aelred, et al. *Aelred of Rievaulx: Spiritual Friendship*. Cistercian Publications, 2010, p.40-41.

[7] Lewis, C. S. *The Four Loves*. HarperOne, 2017, p.58.

[8] Horn, David. *Soulmates: Friendship, Fellowship & the Making of Christian Community*. Hendrickson Publishers, 2017, p.25.

[9] Horn, David. *Soulmates: Friendship, Fellowship & the Making of Christian Community*. Hendrickson Publishers, 2017, p.17.

[10] Lewis, C. S. *The Four Loves*. Harper One, 2017, p.90.

[11] Aelred, et al. *Aelred of Rievaulx: Spiritual Friendship*. Cistercian Publications, 2010, p.33.

CHAPTER VI

[1] Kostenberger, Andreas J. *Baker Exegetical Commentary on the New Testament: John*. Baker Academic, 2004, p.458.

[2] Stein, Robert H. *Mark*. Baker Academic, 2010, p.708-709.

[3] Finley, James. *Merton's Palace of Nowhere*. Ave Maria Press, 2018, p.56.

[4] Finley, James. *Merton's Palace of Nowhere*. Ave Maria Press, 2018, p.57.

[5] Finley, James. *Merton's Palace of Nowhere*. Ave Maria Press, 2018, p.58.

[6] Hall, Douglas John. *The Cross in Our Context: Jesus and the Suffering World*. Fortress Press, 2003, p.54.